Blooming Single, Confidently and Boldly

Tiffany S. Wright

BLOOMING SINGLE, CONFIDENTLY AND BOLDLY.
Copyright © 2023. Tiffany S. Wright. All Rights Reserved.

No rights claimed for public domain material, all rights reserved. No part of this publication may be reproduced, stored in a retrieval system, or transmitted in any form or by any means, electronic, mechanical, photocopying, recording, scanning, or otherwise, without the prior written permission of the publisher. Violation may be subject to civil or criminal penalties.

Scripture quotations marked "KJV" are taken from the Holy Bible, King James Version (Public Domain).

Scripture quotations marked (NIV) are taken from the Holy Bible, New International Version®, NIV®. Copyright © 1973, 1978, 1984 by Biblica, Inc.™ Used by permission of Zondervan. All rights reserved worldwide.

Scripture quotations marked (NLT) are taken from the Holy Bible, New Living Translation, copyright © 1996, 2004, 2007 by Tyndale House Foundation. Used by permission of Tyndale House Publishers, Inc., Carol Stream, Illinois 60188. All rights reserved.

ISBN: 978-1-958404-50-8 (paperback)

Printed in the United States of America

Endorsement

This book comes at a critical time when something of substance needs to be said to those whose dreams of getting married have not yet materialized. This, of course, is from an attractive young woman who herself is waiting and is fully in touch with all the areas of concern for singles.

"Blooming Single" comes at this juncture when marriages in the church are ending in divorce at the same rate as the world, and has damaged our witness of the relationship that exists between Christ and the church. Many relationships in the church no longer reflect the forgiveness and love exemplified by Jesus Christ, and are evident by the increase in separation and divorce. As such, a book like this comes to encourage single men and women to stop putting their lives on hold waiting for Miss Right or the Prince in shining armor, and to be the best version of oneself.

I celebrate the work of Minister Tiffany Wright and her contribution to the archives, and that future generations will understand the things we grapple with in this generation and make better and wiser decisions.

Hats off to you, Tiffany, and may God continue to bless your efforts.

Bishop John Davis
Pastor
Faith Walk Church of God of Prophecy

This book is dedicated to singles, everywhere—
Bloom!

Acknowledgements

God is simply amazing! I am grateful to Him for so ably leading me to pen the words of this book.

Thanks to friends and family who continue to support the projects I embark on, including this one.

Special thanks to my church family at the Faith Walk Church of God of Prophecy, Westchester, led by Bishop John Davis, for holding me up in prayers and for your continuous encouragement and support.

Thanks to my mom, Gloria Dyer, for her constant support and encouragement.

Finally, thanks to you, who are presently reading this book. Thank you for giving me an opportunity to share my thoughts with you.

Table of Contents

Endorsement 3
Acknowledgements 7
Introduction 11
Chapter One: Blooming Single 14
Chapter Two: Grace for the Wait 16
Chapter Three: Know Your Worth 19
Chapter Four: Stronger than Ever 22
Chapter Five: What's Up With This Wait? 24
Chapter Six: I Want to Have Sex 27
Chapter Seven: Lessons From My Single Journey. 32
Chapter Eight: Doll Up, Dress Up and Show Up .. 36
Chapter Nine: Celebrate YOU 39
Chapter Ten: Your Posture Matters 41
Chapter Eleven: Confidence Looks Good on You. 44
Chapter Twelve: What If? 46
Chapter Thirteen: Trust God's Path for Your Life 48
Chapter Fourteen: Surrendering to God's Will 51
Chapter Fifteen: Love Expressions From God 53
    Affirmations 57
    Conclusion 59
    About the Author 61
    Other Books by the Author 63

Introduction

This book is a direct response to the clear instruction by the Lord as He said I needed to get it outside of me as I will not be single for much longer. Now bear in mind, His time and ours are very different, but I am confident that it is just around the corner.

The Barbadians/Bajans have a popular saying, "What doesn't happen in a year, happens in a day." Nothing is impossible with our God. Never stop asking, knocking or seeking. One day you will get an answer; one day the door will be opened, and one day you shall find that which you seek (see Matthew 7:7-8).

I am very much excited and expectant, and I know it will come to pass.

This book is dedicated to all singles who are in your season of waiting, grooming, and blooming. There is hope because our lives are in God, and the core of who God is requires us to exercise faith in His Word.

Don't count me out. God did it for others, He can do it for me. I'm blooming, beaming, and thriving.

I desire to be married and will be one day, but in the interim, I'm going to bloom. Bloom in every area. My husband will find me happy and not waiting on him to enter my life to make me happy. I will exude radiance, light, love, and laughter.

I am whole and complete, lacking nothing, for God has given me everything I need for life and godliness (see 2 Peter 1:3-4).

Being single affords you freedom, so enjoy it and make the most of it. Enjoy not having the responsibilities associated with marriage and taking care of a family. Understand that these are desired, but while I am in this season of waiting, I am determined to live life to the fullest.

Enjoy doing things on your own time at your own leisure. Be intent on enjoying life; travel, try new things, create new memories, and cherish new experiences.

As singles, we have been gifted this time, so let us use it wisely. Now is the time to go back to school, to enroll for that cooking course or events course, to travel, to go on that excursion, to start that business or write that book, and the list goes on.

Now is also the time when you get to earnestly seek God, to find out all you are in Him, all you were created for and to do.

Will you lay around in gloom or will you bloom?

Chapter One
Blooming Single

Absolutely nothing is wrong with you! Yes, there may be areas for improvement, but that does not equate to something being wrong with you and the reasons for you being single.

Married people have things individually and as a couple that they are working on too. Nobody thinks anything is wrong with them, so why should that assumption be made about us? Okay, now that we have settled that, Let's Bloom!

To bloom single is to enjoy life as it is for you now. It is waking up and being grateful, giving thanks for all the things that you have going for you.

It is living your truth, understanding more about who you are each day, and celebrating yourself, toasting yourself, cheering yourself and loving yourself.

It is shining in each area of your life and being the light you were called to be.

Being single is the gift of time. How will you utilize it to your advantage?

Chapter Two
Grace for the Wait

God affords us His grace to help us in times of need.

Not only is grace God's unmerited favour, but it is also His supernatural enablement; that strength that surpasses human ability that gives us the victory when we cannot see how. It is this grace that allows us to wait and trust God's timing.

Ecclesiastes 3 tells us that there is a season for everything, a season to sow and a season to reap, a season of joy and a season of mourning. There is also a season of waiting and a season of breakthrough.

Hang in there.

Your time of singleness requires sacrifice and a call to holiness. This does not mean you and I won't fall. Remember, however, that "there is therefore now no condemnation to them which are in Christ Jesus, who walk not after the flesh, but after the Spirit." (Romans 8:1 - KJV). "What shall we say then? Shall we continue in sin, that grace may abound? God forbid." (Romans 6:1-2 - KJV).

The point is this, we are saved by grace through faith. Not of works lest any man should boast. (Ephesians 2:8-9 - KJV). It means we need His provision of grace daily. We can't do this journey on our own merit or in our own strength.

"And he said unto me, My grace is sufficient for thee: for my strength is made perfect in weakness. Most gladly therefore will I rather glory in my infirmities, that the power of Christ may rest upon me." (2 Corinthians 12:9 - KJV).

He has given unto us everything we need for life and godliness (see 2 Peter 1:3). Know that you are going to be okay.

Enjoy the journey. We are often caught up with arriving at the destination that we miss all that the journey has to offer with its many twists, turns, and surprises.

I promise you, this book is for me just as it is for you. I questioned if I was the right person to even write this, but God affirmed it and reassured me. That was all I needed. In fact, that is all any of us need: the validation and affirmation of the One who created us, the One to whom we belong, the One who has the final say.

Chapter Three
Know Your Worth

Place value on yourself. Only you can determine the extent to which persons acknowledge your worth.

Use this time of singleness to work on you, to be better, sharpen your self-esteem—become the best you that you can be.

Understand the fullness of all that you are, what you have to offer, what you bring to the table.

Know how special you are, how worthy you are, how beautiful you are.

Know you are worth the wait, the chase, the effort, and the spend (Brothers, don't come for me).

Understanding your worth allows you to make good choices and will let you know when to say no or yes. I went on a date once, and it had me in a state of disbelief. The young man came off extremely brash and haughty, which was very unattractive to me.

Though he indicated he was a Christian, nothing about his conversation or demeanour that night convinced me of same. We did not go on a second date.

Further, I was approached at one time to rekindle a past relationship. Now, a lot of thoughts came to mind. My age, for one, and the "biological clock" that is ticking, and I thought to myself, "Will I look back years from now and regret not taking this step?" The result: I could not do it. It would not be God's best for me nor what I truly desire. Faith is hard. Faith is allowing this train to pass and choosing to wait on the other one—the one you hope is coming, but you do not see nor hear.

Knowing your worth takes away panicking or feeling desperate. It allows you to be assured of the decisions you are currently making. It allows you to be at home alone, relaxing, reading a book, or watching a movie and be perfectly okay.

Set the bar for how you want to be treated and spoken to, even in your platonic friendships and even among family members. Create healthy boundaries and realistic standards.

Choose wisely who you spend your time with, who you go on dates with and generally who occupies your space. Your environment matters. Being cultivated in the right soil will allow you to bloom confidently and boldly.

Chapter Four
Stronger than Ever

I honestly believe I am in the best season of my life. I have grown, matured, survived hurricanes, a pandemic, numerous heartbreaks, many disappointments, yet here I am, stronger than ever.

What was meant to take me out has made me stronger, has developed me, and has shaped me. The same is true for you as you read this and reflect. You have your own situations that you can pinpoint to say, "I survived."

I have had my heart broken a few times from relationships and friendships. I have had people walk away and crush my heart in the process. Looking back now, I can admit that those situations have catapulted me right into my destiny. Just like Joseph, what the enemy meant for evil, God turned it around for my good.

Kelly Clarkson, in her song *Stronger,* says "What doesn't kill you makes you stronger." Use each experience to learn, grow, and be better.

Now, it is time to thrive!
Nothing can hold me back.
Nothing can hold you back.
Let's go bloom!

Chapter Five
What's Up With This Wait?

Psalm 27:14 states "Wait on the Lord: be of good courage, and he shall strengthen thine heart: wait, I say, on the Lord." (KJV).

Let's be honest; waiting is not easy. We have microwaves to get our food heated up quickly. We look for the express lines in the supermarkets, and we take the tag lane of the toll to avoid long lines to get to our destinations much quicker.

We are wired to get things NOW. So, when we are met with a situation that requires waiting, it pulls on us. It takes discipline, faith, and courage to continue waiting, especially over an extended period.

Romans 5:4-6 speaks of patience producing character and character hope. "Hope," I am loving this word more each day. "for hope maketh not ashamed, because the love of God is shed abroad in our hearts…" (Romans 5:5 – KJV).

Romans 8:25 states "…then do we with patience wait for it." (KJV). My take-away is that we must keep hope alive. Whatever we are believing for, don't stop believing and expecting to see it manifest.

The scripture in Psalm 27:14 indicates that while we wait, God will strengthen our hearts. Waiting is a process, and there may be times along the journey when we get daunted or disheartened, but here we are told God will indeed **strengthen** us.

"Be of good courage…" (Psalm 27:14 – KJV). Be brave and courageous as you continue to wait. Courage does not come amidst easy circumstances. Courage is executed during hard and challenging times. So, stand tall as you wait, despite the criticisms that may come, the disappointments you may face, and the mistakes you may make, "Be of good courage."

Isaiah 40:31: "But they that wait upon the Lord shall renew their strength; they shall mount up with wings as eagles; they shall run, and not be weary; and they shall walk, and not faint." (KJV).

There is beauty in waiting. Don't move without God; wait on Him. Isaiah 30:18 declares, "Blessed are all those who wait for Him." (NKJV).

Further, Isaiah 49:23 says "for they shall not be ashamed that wait for me." (KJV). The **NIV** of the same verse says, "those who hope in me will not be disappointed."

Wait and hope; hope and wait. Now this "hope" is not wishful thinking, it is an active stance whereby you are standing on the Word of God, believing and exercising your faith for that which you have committed to Him to come to pass.

…Christ in you, the **hope** of glory (Colossians 1:27 - KJV).

Chapter Six
I Want to Have Sex

Yes, you heard correctly. I want to have sex!

I wish we would start to be open and have these conversations often. I do believe we would save a lot of persons some heartaches if we spoke more about sex in Christendom.

Wanting to have sex is normal and natural. Feeling turned on in the presence of someone you are attracted to is normal and natural; even feeling this way outside of the presence of someone you are attracted to is normal. It is how we handle this that makes the difference.

It is natural, simple. God made us this way.

Longing to be touched, held, kissed, and made love to are all natural human desires. We were made to have these needs; hence, God created the opposite sex with whom we can share intimacy with and fulfil these needs and desires.

Church and church culture have kept some of us so sheltered that we really have no clue when it comes to sex, which causes our curiosity to pique, which sometimes takes us on a path of searching and researching, which usually ends in us slipping up more often than not. We get so caught up with wanting to know more that we get hooked on porn sites or decide to experiment on our own. I believe an injustice has been done where the church refusing to talk on, or shying away from the topic of sex, has done more harm than good.

Is purity still relevant in the 21st century, one might ask. It sure is! Purity will always be relevant as God's Word remains constant. It has not changed and will not change.

Sex should be pleasurable but not cheap. I was struggling with deciding to have sex at one point, and God dropped this in my spirit, and I was like, wow. Needless to say, this totally got me back in line!

We are admonished in 2 Timothy 2:22 to "Flee also youthful lusts: but follow righteousness, faith, charity, peace, with them that call on the Lord out of a pure heart." (KJV).

A desire to honour the temple of the Holy Spirit must be what is paramount in our hearts and minds as we discuss the matter of purity (see 1 Corinthians 6:19-20). Now, honouring the temple also relates to how we eat, the rest we get, how often we exercise, but seeing we are on the topic of sex, then that is our focus.

We are not perfect, and we do get into situations that cause us to fall at times, but the resolve is to not enter those situations. However, be reminded, you are not condemned if you fall (see Romans 8:1). Notwithstanding, we are encouraged to take the necessary steps to not be in situations that will cause such an outcome.

Thankfully, all is not lost. We know that God is able to make a way of escape if temptation comes knocking.

"There hath no temptation taken you but such as is common to man: but God is faithful, who will not suffer you to be tempted above that ye are able; but will with the temptation also make a way to escape, that ye may be able to bear it." (1 Corinthians 10:13 – KJV).

Tips for Purity

- Accountability is KEY. Having someone to talk with and to hold yourself accountable to is a great tool for maintaining your purity.

- Setting boundaries is crucial. Know your weaknesses, set time limits, decide beforehand where a date will be and what the expectations are; what will and will not happen.

- Sign up with a counsellor for pre-marital counselling, even while you are single. Especially if you do not have any or much sexual experience. I believe it will help you tremendously. Firstly, in managing expectations; secondly, in handling the curiosity that comes with wanting to explore and, finally, in preparing you for marriage and improving your existing relationships with family members, friends, church family or at work. (Full transparency. I am yet to do this as the Holy Spirit dropped this in my spirit at the time of writing this book).

- Having a made-up mind is powerful and cannot be stressed enough. Joseph made up in his mind that he would not sin against God (see Genesis 39:9).

- Remind yourself of God's Word, your commitment to Him, and your desire to please Him.

- Pray intensely in the times you are strong. When you are weak, it will be hard to utter a prayer or you may not even want to pray, so pray in advance.

Chapter Seven
Lessons From My Single Journey

There are some lessons I have learnt on this journey that I would like to share with you. Some I have learnt from others, and the rest through my own experiences.

1. You are not starting over. You are gaining experience and moving forward. When you experience a break-up, take the lessons and move forward. It may feel like you are starting over, but you are not. You are more focused, more resilient, more mature, and more ready than you were before. Try again. You will be better for it.

2. Talk about things you are uncomfortable with from early in the dating process, and do not be afraid to be your authentic self.

3. Wait for the one who will wait for you (sex after marriage). Don't be rushed, and if someone is unable to wait, they are NOT the one.

4. Prepare/develop yourself. Study, exercise, **practice**: sharpen skills such as cooking, etc.

5. Save and Invest. Clear your debts as best as you can. Increase your savings and investments. Get financially sound/stable.

6. Go on dates. This is how you will know what is out there, who is for you and who is not.

7. Continue to hope and believe. Never give up!

8. Maintain and treasure your friendships, especially those friends who never cease to pray for and encourage you.

9. Live while you are waiting. Enjoy life.

10. Do not compromise your belief/value system. Though we are learning more, and we are downloading new revelations from God, some things are foundational and are rooted and grounded. For example, I believe in the virgin birth, death, burial, and resurrection of Jesus Christ. I am not going to be dating someone who is of a different belief, and who would want to debate this truth. I dated someone once (very briefly) who did not

believe in the giving of tithes and offerings. Tithes is one thing, but offerings? He said he believed in giving to a cause, but he is not giving to the Lord because the Lord has no use for money. Listen! I am not doing it. #MovingRightAlong

11. Don't be afraid to share your struggles. Talk it out, share disappointments, annoyances, etc. Understand that your experiences can help someone, and through these conversations, you may find encouragement for yourself as well.

12. Learn to trust again. Forgive those who have hurt you. Be wise in your interactions, friendships and relationships, but do not close off your heart because of the hurt you have experienced. Learn to love again and be open to new experiences that can easily flourish into so much more.

13. Connect with others. Hang out with other singles. Spend time around couples as well to learn by observation what that dynamic looks like. Sign up for and attend single seminars or seminars that are geared towards improving relationships.

14. Pour into others. This can take many forms; be creative. Taking the focus off your needs and attending to others not only helps them but also you. There is joy in serving, so while you wait, serve. The Bible says it best "…it is more blessed to give than to receive." (Acts 20:35 - KJV).

15. Worship. Maintain intimacy with God. Entertain His presence—live in it, breathe it, honour it.

16. Cultivate an active prayer life. Your prayer life is crucial in every step of your life and, most certainly, for your single journey.

17. Remember, you are deserving of love and are completely accepted and loved by God.

Chapter Eight
Doll Up, Dress Up and Show Up

It took me a while to get into the "doll up" league but better late than never.

We must "put" ourselves together and enhance what God has already blessed us with.

I would start with a pleasant countenance. "A cheerful heart is good medicine, but a broken spirit saps a person's strength." (Proverbs 17:22 - NLT). Be pleasant to approach (smile) and be around. No one wants to be around someone who is miserable or in a funky mood all the time.

Laugh!

Proverbs 15:13 says, "A glad heart makes a happy face; a broken heart crushes the spirit." (NLT).

Women from the Caribbean are very "strong," and we can come off as being aggressive at times. Fortunately, we can address this by simply being mindful of the things that bring out this kind of behaviour and learn how to taper it. Too much aggression can be a turn off.

Now, for the other aspects. Get your hair and nails done (well-kept and clean thereafter), dress attractively and currently, smell good, add make-up or, if you are not a make-up person, use lip gloss/balm. What you want to ensure is that you are stepping out confidently and boldly like the gem that you are.

I encourage you to do your dental and doctor check-ups. Eat well and get enough sleep. Take care of YOU.

We read in Esther 2 that before any woman was brought into the king, she had to go through one year of beauty purification; six months with oil of myrrh and another six months in perfumes and oils. My take-away is that we are to pamper and take care of ourselves. Find avenues to relax and rejuvenate. Get rid of the tension in your muscles. Exercising can also help with this. These help in how we feel on the inside, which ultimately will extend to our countenance externally.

Of course, to each his own. Whatever makes you feel at your optimal, the point is to be conscious that appearance matters and that, just as you are looking for Mr. Tall Dark and Handsome (well-groomed and sharp), he is also looking for Miss Gorgeous.

Chapter Nine
Celebrate YOU

Celebrate your achievements, your awesomeness, small things, big things, anything, and everything.

Compliment yourself. You will begin to hear it so often from yourself that it won't be necessary to hear it from others. Often when I get dressed, I look in the mirror and say, "Tiff, you're looking really nice."

Celebrate yourself. No "poor me" attitude around here or "woe is me."

Mental health became prominent during the Corona Virus pandemic as many persons battled depression due to the lockdowns, etc. It became even more necessary to ensure that individually we are taking care of ourselves and looking out for ourselves. David encouraged himself in the Lord. We must do the same.

Take time out to treat yourself. Improve the happy cells of the brain—whatever puts a smile on your face. Is it watching a movie? Walking along the seashore? Having ice-cream? Talking to a friend? Taking a trip? Whatever happy looks like for you, make room for it, often.

One of my friends has a business that is built upon celebrating just about everything. She calls herself a *Life Celebrator.* We all should be one as we choose to celebrate our wins, no matter how small.

Live life out loud—confidently and boldly!

Chapter Ten
Your Posture Matters

Ruth gets her husband (see Ruth 2).

The story of Ruth, though seemingly exhausted (especially when us females talk about "finding our Boaz"), cannot be overlooked. Ruth was busy, serving her God, living her life, working her money, minding her business, when she caught the eyes of Boaz.

Lesson: Focus. Live. Achieve.

Do not just sit around idly waiting; be actively waiting. Love on your God, carry out your purpose, sharpen your skills, and live in *faith* believing God is going to exceed your expectations.

He has done it. He can do it. He will do it.

Isaac gets his wife (see Genesis 24).

Abraham sent his servant to find a wife for Isaac. The servant prayed a very specific prayer, and it happened just as he asked.

Genesis 24:14, "And let it come to pass, that the damsel to whom I shall say, Let down thy pitcher, I pray thee, that I may drink; and she shall say, Drink, and I will give thy camels drink also: let the same be she that thou hast appointed for thy servant Isaac; and thereby shall I know that thou hast shewed kindness unto my master." (KJV).

We see the manifestation of this declaration in Genesis 24:18-19. Listen! Pray for exactly what you want. It can happen exactly as you have asked. Go ahead and ask!

Lesson: Make your request(s) known to God. Ensure you truly want what you are asking for as you will receive just that.

Philippians 4:6-7, "Do not be anxious about anything, but in every situation, by prayer and petition, with thanksgiving, present your requests to God. And the peace of God, which transcends all understanding, will guard your hearts and your minds in Christ Jesus." (NIV).

Our posture should be one where we are not grumbling or complaining but "in everything, giving thanks for this is the will of God in Christ Jesus concerning you." (1 Thessalonians 5:18 – KJV).

Keep praying.
Keep worshipping.
Keep believing.
Your posture matters.

Chapter Eleven
Confidence Looks Good on You

Expect pressure from society, family, and friends, but learn to respond and/react accordingly with grace. When you expect it, you are better able to handle it. Be confident in who you are and where you are, and know that whatever the result, it is working out for your good (see Romans 8:28). Use these opportunities to remind others of this too. Remind them that your trust is in God and you are trusting Him to continue to order your steps.

Affirm yourself in the perfect will of God. He is in charge and, ultimately, you are choosing to walk in His perfect will for your life. I am sure, like me, you have been tempted with other options, but you KNOW they are not in the will of God for your life. Stand confidently and boldly in what you believe.

Keep a positive outlook. Encourage yourself. Speak over yourself and to yourself. God has NOT forgotten you.

Ensure you continue to speak the Word of God. If you are like me, there are times when moments of doubt creep in, and you start to waver in faith, but I am always brought back on track as I remind myself of God's promises which are yea and amen (see 2 Corinthians 1:20). God is able.

It is His Word that builds my confidence. It is what has kept me.

Confidence looks good on you. Wear it boldly.

Chapter Twelve
What If?

What if you never get married? Is it the end of the world? Absolutely not!

I listened to a eulogy a few months ago of this community builder. What struck me as the eulogy was being read was that she had no biological children, but she had adopted sons. Her impact was no less because she did not biologically have children. Her sons praised her nonetheless. She gave, she served, she lived. Yes, she was married, but again, we assume we know how the story will end as the assumption is that getting married means we will automatically have children. This is not the case for many. My take-away: LIVE! Married, single, divorced, widowed, just LIVE. Make a mark and leave an impact.

Believe me, this has been the hardest book to write as I thought by now, I would be married with children, but when I think of it, had I been married say five years ago, I may not have had the time or the experiences that have shaped me into penning three books prior to this one. It could possibly mean that I would not have started my business, or I may not have made the career and educational moves I made that opened so many doors for me, including meaningful and valuable friendships.

I am so clear on my purpose and what God has called me to do because I have had the blessing of my single years to know and learn more about myself, and to grow more intimately with God. Don't get me wrong, I am not saying married persons are denied this, but being single is my vantage point.

We cannot be hung up on what ifs. We must trust God and believe that He is ordering our steps every step of the way. We must know it is working for our good, eventually, whether we see it in the present moment or not.

"For I know the plans I have for you…" (Jeremiah 29:11 – NIV).

He knows, so RELAX.

Chapter Thirteen
Trust God's Path for Your Life

"Trust in the Lord with all thine heart; and lean not to thy own understanding. In all thy ways acknowledge him, and he shall direct thy paths." (Proverbs 3:5-6 - KJV).

We must trust the path He is taking us on—the journey He is using to ensure we come out like pure gold, to ensure we look more like Jesus every day.

His Word is a lamp unto our feet and a light unto our path (Psalm 119:105 - KJV). We have a blessed assurance that though we may walk through the valley of the shadow of death, God's protection and guidance is ever-present.

The writer of Ecclesiastes tells us that there is a time for everything. Isaiah 60:22 further declares, "At the right time, I, the Lord, will make it happen." (NLT). Therefore, it behoves us to allow the Lord to do His work in our lives "being predestined according to the purpose of Him who works all things according to the counsel of His will." (Ephesians 1:11 - NKJV).

God's got this!

God—the all-knowing, all-sovereign One—already sees the end of our journey here on earth; what it looks like, and who we will be. We, therefore, really have no choice but to trust Him as He, through the Holy Spirit, shows us how to navigate the things that will come at us, that is, of course, if we desire to stay in His perfect will for our lives.

One of my confidants consistently reminds me of this truth, "The steps of a good man are ordered by the Lord: and he delighteth in his way." (Psalm 37:23 - KJV).

Your steps are ordered. This means time has not run out on you. You are at the right place and at the right time. You have not missed your window of opportunity.

Stay the course.

I read somewhere: "They tell us to trust the process, but what if the process doesn't know we are trusting it?" I chuckled because I totally understood the sentiment behind the question. Sometimes, we are trusting "the process" by doing all we know how to do, and yet things often go in the opposite direction than the one we envisioned.

To this, I would say, trust the One who is in control of the process. He is working it out for you. Period.

Chapter Fourteen
Surrendering to God's Will

No good thing will He withhold from those who walk uprightly.

Surrendering is not EASY, especially If you are as analytical as I am, but we must remember that God, our Father, knows what our future looks like.

We must surrender to His perfect will for our lives. Not our will, but His will be done.

Surrendering to God's will can come off very cliché at times, but it is required. We must surrender; yield to the higher call upon our lives.

I separated this topic from the one that preceded it because surrendering and trusting, though similar, are different. I can trust to a point; so far and no more. I can also trust in one area and not in another. For example, I can trust that God will provide for me financially but not trust that He will heal me, but when I surrender, I give up my right, choice, will, thoughts—everything—and submit them to Him. I literally am not my own but now allow the Holy

Spirit to lead and rule on my behalf because, yes, now I trust Him 100%.

Sometimes we must get out of our own heads and over ourselves and realize that not everything is about us (Ouch! Don't worry, that hit me first). There is a far greater purpose to our destiny than the fulfilment of our needs. We have a generation to impact and influence to ensure that they reflect the Kingdom of the One who called us out of darkness into His marvelous light (see 1 Peter 2:9).

We are charged in Matthew 6:33, "But seek first his kingdom and his righteousness, and all these things will be given to you as well." (NIV).

Provision has already been made for that which we need, so why not surrender?

Chapter Fifteen
Love Expressions From God

Gary Chapman's *5 Love Languages* have been used to set the tone in many relationships, as couples, especially, have been exposed to things they were probably already doing as expressions of love or things they desire from their partner that would make them feel loved. The *5 Love Languages,* as shared by Chapman, are: acts of service, physical touch, gifts, quality time, and words of affirmation.

While we use these languages to better our relationships with each other, I want to remind us that absolutely no one can love us more than God, the Father, expressed through the sacrifice of His Son. No one knows us more deeply and intimately. I have selected a few scriptures to further remind us just how intentional Abba is about each of us and, ultimately, how His heart is towards us.

O lord, thou hast searched me, and known me. Thou knowest my downsitting and mine uprising, thou understandest my thought afar off. Thou compassest my path and my lying down, and art acquainted with all my ways. For there is not a word in my tongue, but, lo, O Lord, thou knowest it altogether. Thou hast beset me behind and before, and laid thine hand upon me. Such knowledge is too wonderful for me; it is high, I cannot attain unto it. Whither shall I go from thy spirit? or whither shall I flee from thy presence? If I ascend up into heaven, thou art there: if I make my bed in hell, behold, thou art there. If I take the wings of the morning, and dwell in the uttermost parts of the sea; Even there shall thy hand lead me, and thy right hand shall hold me. If I say, Surely the darkness shall cover me; even the night shall be light about me. Yea, the darkness hideth not from thee; but the night shineth as the day: the darkness and the light are both alike to thee. For thou hast possessed my reins: thou hast covered me in my mother's womb. I will praise thee; for I am fearfully and wonderfully made: marvellous are thy works; and that my soul knoweth right well. My substance was not hid from thee, when I was made in secret, and curiously wrought in the lowest parts of the earth. Thine eyes did see my substance, yet being unperfect; and in thy book all my members were written, which in continuance were fashioned, when as yet there was none of them. How precious also are thy thoughts unto me, O God! how great is the sum of them! If I should count them, they are more in number than the sand: when I awake, I am still with thee. (Psalm 139:1-18 - KJV).

The Lord hath appeared of old unto me, saying, Yea, I have loved thee with an everlasting love: therefore with lovingkindness have I drawn thee. (Jeremiah 31:3 - KJV).

"Though the mountains be shaken and the hills be removed, yet my unfailing love for you will not be shaken nor my covenant of peace be removed," says the Lord, who has compassion on you. (Isaiah 54:10 - NIV).

In this was manifested the love of God toward us, because that God sent his only begotten Son into the world, that we might live through him. Herein is love, not that we loved God, but that he loved us, and sent his Son to be the propitiation for our sins. (1 John 4:9-10 - KJV)

For God so loved the world, that he gave his only begotten Son, that whosoever believeth in him should not perish, but have everlasting life. (John 3:16 - KJV).

For I am persuaded, that neither death, nor life, nor angels, nor principalities, nor powers, nor things present, nor things to come, nor height, nor depth, nor any other creature, shall be able to separate us from the love of God, which is in Christ Jesus our Lord. (Romans 8:38-39 - KJV).

But God commendeth his love toward us, in that, while we were yet sinners, Christ died for us. (Romans 5:8 - KJV).

But God, who is rich in mercy, for his great love wherewith he loved us, Even when we were dead in sins, hath quickened us together with Christ, (by grace ye are saved;) (Ephesians 2:4-5 - KJV).

Before I formed thee in the belly I knew thee; and before thou camest forth out of the womb I sanctified thee, and I ordained thee a prophet unto the nations. (Jeremiah 1:5 - KJV).

Blessed be the Lord, Who daily loads us with benefits, The God of our salvation! Selah. (Psalm 68:19 - NKJV).

Affirmations

We all crave affirmations at some point or another. We cannot however leave it up to others to affirm us; that may never come. We must do it ourselves. Here are a few of mine:

- I am 100% committed to God's will for my life.
- I am whole and complete, lacking nothing.
- I am blessed in every area of my life.
- I am worthy of love.
- I am lovable.
- I am loved.
- I am attractive.
- I am beautiful.
- I am intelligent.
- I am a winner.
- I am royalty.
- I am confident.
- I am forgiven.
- I am chosen.
- I am accepted.
- I am as bold as a lion.
- I am an overcomer.

- I am living. I am thriving. I am blooming.

_____
_____
_____
_____
_____
_____
_____
_____
_____
_____
_____
_____
_____
_____
_____
_____
_____
_____

Go ahead and add to this list.

Read them over often as a constant reminder of your value and worth.

Conclusion

All to Jesus I surrender,
All to Him I freely give:
I will ever love and trust Him,
In His presence daily Live.

I surrender all,
I surrender all,
All to Thee, my blessed Savior
I surrender all.

This is a verse and chorus from the popular hymn "All to Jesus I surrender." I pray that this will become our anthem and vow as we continue along the journey God has set before us, knowing He is the Author and Finisher of our faith (see Hebrews 12:2). Anything He starts, He will complete (see Philippians 1:6). He is perfecting that which concerns us (see Psalm 138:8).

God wants the best for us, and, more importantly, He knows what is best for us.

Now, let's go bloom, confidently and boldly!

Notes

About the Author

Tiffany Wright is a Kingdom Strategist called to ensure Christ is well represented on the earth. She is Jamaican-born and has been a member of the Church of God of Prophecy since 1999. Her guided philosophy is: "For in Him we live, and move, and have our being." (Acts 17:28).

She holds a Bachelor of Science Degree in Management Studies (Marketing Major) from The University of the West Indies, and a Master of Science Degree in Marketing and Data Analytics from The Mona School of Business & Management, The University of the West Indies.

Tiffany is the founder and CEO of God's Brand Collections, a locally operated business that is grounded on Matthew 5:16, "Let your light so shine before men, that they may see your good works, and glorify your Father which is in Heaven." (KJV).

Tiffany is an ordained Minister of Religion.

She can be contacted at tiffanywrightcool@gmail.com or IG @blessed_tiffs or @godsbrand_collections

Other Books by the Author
(Available on Amazon)

www.ingramcontent.com/pod-product-compliance
Lightning Source LLC
Chambersburg PA
CBHW060857050426
42453CB00008B/997